Communication Between Different Worlds

By Annie Besant

ISBN: 978-1-63118-569-4

Esoteric Classics

Other Books in this Series and Related Titles

Aurora of the Philosophers by Paracelsus (978-1-63118-507-6)

Clairvoyance and Psychic Abilities by A Besant &c (978-1-63118-403-1)

The Feminine Occult by various authors (978-1-63118-711-7)

Rosicrucian Rules, Secret Signs, Codes and Symbols by various (978-1-63118-488-8)

An Outline of Theosophy by C W Leadbeater (978-1-63118-452-9)

Paracelsus, the Four Elements and Their Spirits by M P Hall (978-1-63118-400-0)

Essays on Ancient Magic by Helena P Blavatsky (978-1-63118-535-9)

Essays on the Esoteric Tradition of Karma by A Besant &c (978-1-63118-426-0)

The Use of Evil by Annie Besant (978-1-63118-532-8)

The Alchemical Catechism of Paracelsus by Paracelsus (978-1-63118-513-7)

Alchemy in the Nineteenth Century by Helena P Blavatsky (978-1-63118-446-8)

Qabbalistic Teachings and the Tree of Life by M P Hall (978-1-63118-482-6)

The Historic, Mythic and Mystic Christ by Annie Besant (978–1–63118–533–5)

The Hidden Mysteries of Christianity by Annie Besant (978–1–63118–534–2)

History, Analysis and Secret Tradition of the Tarot by Hall &c (978-1-63118-445-1)

Crystal Vision Through Crystal Gazing by Frater Achad (978-1-63118-455-0)

The Golden Verses of Pythagoras: Five Translations (978-1-63118-479-6)

Arcane Formulas or Mental Alchemy by W W Atkinson (978-1-63118-459-8)

The Machinery of the Mind by Dion Fortune (978-1-63118-451-2)

The A E Waite Reader: A Selection of Occult Essays (978-1-63118-515-1)

The Leadbeater Reader: A Selection of Occult Essays (978-1-63118-483-3)

Audio versions are also available on Audible, Amazon and Apple

Other Books in this Series and Related Titles

Animism, Magic and the Omnipotence of Thought by S Freud (978–1–63118–568–7)

Buddhism by F Otto Schrader (978–1–63118–567–0)

Death by W W Westcott (978–1–63118–566–3)

The Religion of Theosophy by Bhagwan Das (978–1–63118–565–6)

The Spirit of Zoroastrianism by Henry S Olcott (978–1–63118–564–9)

The Brotherhood of Religions by Annie Besant (978–1–63118–563–2)

Fourth Book of Maccabees by Josephus (978-1-63118-562-5)

The Story of Ahikar by Ahiqar (978-1-63118-561-8)

Vision of the Spirit by C. Jinarajadasa (978-1-63118-560-1)

Occult Arts by William Q. Judge (978-1-63118-559-5)

Kali the Mother by Sister Nivedita (978-1-63118-558-8)

Love and Death by Sri Aurobindo (978–1–63118–557–1)

Times and Seasons Volume 1, Numbers 4-6 (978-1-63118-556-4)

Times and Seasons Volume 1, Numbers 1-3 (978-1-63118-555-7)

The Book of John Whitmer by John Whitmer (978-1-63118-554-0)

Interesting Account of Several Remarkable Visions (978-1-63118-553-3)

The Evening and Morning Star Volume 1, Numbers 11 & 12 (978-1-63118-552-6)

The Evening and Morning Star Volume 1, Numbers 1 & 2 (978-1-63118-547-2)

Private Diary of Joseph Smith 1832-1834 (978-1-63118-546-5)

An Address to All Believers in Christ Elder David Whitmer (978-1-63118-545-8)

A Manuscript on Far West by Reed Peck (978-1-63118-544-1)

Audio versions are also available on Audible, Amazon and Apple

Table of Contents

INTRODUCTION

The word "esoteric" can be difficult to define. Esotericism in general can be seen less as a system of beliefs and more as a category, which encompasses numerous, different systems of beliefs. It's a bit of juxtaposition, since the word "esoteric" indicates something that few people know about, while the term itself broadly covers numerous philosophies, practices, areas of study and belief systems.

In a greater sense, Esotericism acts as a storehouse for secret knowledge, which is often considered ancient (by *tradition, if not by fact),* passed down from generation to generation, in private. At various times in history, simply possessing the knowledge of some of these subjects, was considered illegal and a jailable offence, if discovered. This usually included such general topics as Alchemy, Pharmacology, Qabalah, Hermeticism, Occultism, Ceremonial Magic, Astrology, Divination, Rosicrucianism and so on. Collectively, these areas of study were often referred to as the esoteric sciences.

Sometimes, the outer garment of a subject isn't esoteric, while what is hidden beneath it, is. As an example, Freemasonry isn't necessarily esoteric by nature (at *least not anymore),* but certain signs, passwords and handshakes given to the candidate during their initiation, are in fact, esoteric, in the sense that they are hidden from the general public.

Today, in the twenty-first century, such topics are readily available at bookstores across the country, and numerous main-steam publishers offer beginners guides and coffee-table volumes on many of these subjects, intended for mass appeal. Books like "*The Secret*" have turned previously arcane topics into household knowledge. All that being the case, however, it isn't to say that there still aren't buried secrets to uncover, ancient wisdom being ignored and forgotten mysteries to be explored. In fact, it is often that we are only able to further our own studies by standing on the shoulders of these disappearing giants.

Lamp of Trismegistus is doing its part to help preserve humanity's esoteric history by making some of these classics available to those students who are seeking to unearth the knowledge of these ancient colossi.

So, be sure to check other titles from our *Esoteric Classics* series, as well as our *Occult Fiction*, *Theosophical Classics*, *Foundations of Freemasonry Series*, *Supernatural Fiction*, *Paranormal Research Series*, *Studies in Buddhism* and our *Christian Apocrypha Series.* You can also download the audio versions of most of these titles from Amazon, Apple or Audible, for learning on the go.

COMMUNICATION BETWEEN DIFFERENT WORLDS

By Annie Besant

THE Theosophical Society is differentiated from most of the religious movements of the day by asserting the continuance in our own time of communication between the different worlds in which humanity is living. All religions assert that such communication took place in the past; they all claim for their Founders, and generally for their associates and immediate followers, that such communication was enjoyed, and enabled them to "speak with authority"; some, as the Hindû and the Roman Catholic, allege that in sporadic cases scattered through their respective histories such communication was established, though rarely, if ever, found today. But the Theosophical Society definitely asserts the existence of powers which lie latent in all men, and of the forces in nature that are as yet hidden from common knowledge, and makes it one of its objects to study these. Some of its members have so successfully followed these studies as to evoke these powers and control these forces, using methods taught by the Masters of the WISDOM, whereby such communication may be normally established and carried on, without provoking the difficulties and disadvantages embarrassing the methods known as spiritualistic. The latter remain, however, as the only methods within the immediate use of the untrained, and hence are of the greatest value in destroying the prejudices of the scientist and the materialist, and in giving physical and tangible proofs, available to every one, of the continuity of consciousness through death. They are a sign of the changing age through which the world is passing, a herald of the approaching era in which the barrier of death will be broken down, the invisible become the visible, and the physical and astral worlds will intermingle.

In order thoroughly to understand the subject before us, it is necessary to grasp certain fundamental laws of nature; when these are clearly seen, it is comparatively easy to apply them to special cases that may come under our notice. And it must be remembered, in order that this study may be useful, that all fear of the unusual must be put aside; the student must realize that there are many things around him which he does not see, and that they become less dangerous, though sometimes more alarming, when they pass from invisibility into visibility. It is the unknown which may be dangerous; it is ignorance which is full of fears. The child unused to strangers screams and hides its face in its mother's dress at the terrifying sight of a harmless man or woman; accustomed to such meetings, the child has no fear. The sight of a ghost startles on the first occasion; after awhile they are no more alarming than the sight of a passing stranger in the street. Our ignorance is our real danger, and that can only be gotten rid of by experience. A reasonable and thoughtful person, pure of life and bright of intelligence, may train himself for normal communication with other worlds without any danger worthy of consideration, provided that he is habitually self-controlled, deliberate and energetic; such a one may evolve himself rationally and quietly, and not only convince himself of the reality of other worlds, but may become a source of help and comfort to others lessening and even removing their fear of death, and softening the anguish of separation from their beloved. Such a person normally guards himself in the physical world, where danger is far more potent than in subtler worlds, because dense physical matter is far more resistant to control by thought than is the subtle matter of higher worlds. Human power of self-defense against danger is smallest in the physical world; in other worlds fear is the worst enemy, because it paralyses thought and will. I do not say there are no dangers in the subtler worlds; dangers there are; but the more we know the more are we safe, and there are dangers for the ignorant everywhere.

The first fundamental fact is that each individual is a single consciousness, a unit of consciousness, and that varieties in the form of communication arise from difference of bodies, not from difference of consciousness. A consciousness may, of course, be more or less unfolded, may have brought into manifestation more or less of his powers; one unit of consciousness may differ widely from another unit; but the same unit, i.e., the same individual, remains the same in all communications, however restricted or unrestricted by the particular body, gross or fine, through which the communication is made. If we compare two units of consciousness, one advanced and one backward, the difference in evolution will be marked in each world in which they function; but the manifestation of each will be determined by the material conditions of manifestation, and these will introduce a variety in the form of communication, but will not affect the unity of the manifesting intelligence. It is well also to bear in mind that all consciousness are fragments, parts, of the one all-pervading consciousness, and hence their characteristics are fundamentally the same, however differing in degree; all will possess the three essential attributes of Will, Wisdom and Activity, though Will may only have reached the point of unfoldment at which we call it Desire, though Wisdom may be seen only in its embryonic form of Cognition, and though Activity may be only manifested in the shape of Restlessness. There are no essential differences in the units of consciousness trying to manifest themselves in various worlds; but there are innumerable differences in degree, from the mighty and luminous consciousness of the highest seraph to the dim and scarcely even groping consciousness in the mineral. There is but one consciousness in the universe and all so-called separated consciousness are phases thereof.

The second fundamental fact is that these units of consciousness are embodied, i.e., are closely related to portions of matter which they have temporarily appropriated. For the purposes of our study we need not concern ourselves with the highest of these appropriations; we may content ourselves with recognizing the fact that there are finer grades of matter than those to which here we confine ourselves, and may indicate these by the general term of the spiritual body without further particularizing them. Those who can freely use the spiritual body are certainly not in need of any explanations such as those given in this article. We are concerned, then, only with three well-defined grades of matter, those which answer to, and are the instruments of, thought, desire and action — mental, astral and physical. From the mental matter is organized the mental body; from the astral matter the astral body; from the physical matter the physical body, which is functionally divisible into its etheric and gross parts. These are the vehicles, the instruments of the unit of consciousness, his means of affecting, and being affected by, the outer worlds in which he lives; these may be highly or poorly organized, may be composed of fine or coarse materials; such as they are, they are his only means of contact with the worlds surrounding him, and his only means of self-expression. These three bodies — mental, astral, and physical — are separable from each other, and under abnormal conditions the two parts of the physical body may to some extent be dissociated during physical life, and are completely dissociated at physical death. While a man is awake and in his ordinary every-day state of consciousness, he is using these three bodies all the time; when he goes to sleep he leaves the physical body, and uses only two — the astral and mental; at death, the grosser part of the physical drops away, the finer part clinging to him for a short period (normally), and then dropping away from him as did the grosser part, and he uses only the astral and mental bodies in the post-mortem condition for a period varying in length; later, the astral body also drops away from him, and he remains clothed in the mental body during the long mental, or heavenly life, intervening between the intermediate state and rebirth into the physical world. When this also drops away from him, he finds himself on the threshold of reincarnation, of the building of new bodies for his next period of physical life.

The third fundamental fact is that man is living, functioning, in three worlds during the waking periods of his life on earth. These three worlds are the worlds composed severally of physical, astral and mental matter, the worlds from which are severally drawn the materials for his physical, astral, and mental bodies. These worlds are not separate from each other, but interpenetrate and intermingle, while remaining distinct. Just as gas may pass into water but remains distinct from it, so does astral matter interpenetrate physical matter while remaining distinct from it, and so does mental matter, being still finer, interpenetrate the astral. Physical ether interpenetrates the gases, liquids and solids of the physical body, moving through every part of it unhindered; so does superphysical matter interpenetrate physical, moving unhindered through every part of it by reason of its greater subtlety. Nature everywhere repeats herself, and we may understand much of the superphysical by studying the physical and reasoning by analogy; but we must ever remember that the superphysical is the original and the physical the copy, and not vice versa. The astral world, while intermingling with the physical, is not conterminous with it; it forms a sphere round the sphere of the earth, and a radius of this astral sphere would extend from the center of our earth to the moon. The mental, or heavenly world, again, is a similar concentric sphere, stretching far beyond the limits of the astral, although interpenetrating both it and the physical. According to the development of the respective bodies will be a man's consciousness of each world; as a man physically blind cannot see the physical world which stretches around him, so a man astrally blind cannot see the astral world though it ever environs him; similarly may a man whose astral sight is open, be mentally blind and fail to see the mental world encompassing him. The matter in each body must be organized in order that consciousness may use it as an instrument of perception; the physically blind, at the present stage of evolution, are a small minority; the astrally blind are a huge majority; but blindness of organisms does not change the worlds in which they live — except to themselves. Thus men are living in three worlds at every moment of their waking consciousness, though normally conscious only of the densest; in sleep and after death, they are living in two, but are normally conscious only of the intermediate world, and not always of that; at a later period of their postmortem condition they are living in only one, and conscious but of their immediate surroundings in that. As evolution proceeds, the astral world will become visible to those who occupy the crest of the wave of normally advancing humanity, and at a far future time, the mental will also become visible, so that men on earth will live consciously in the three worlds, the three bodies having become organized as vehicles of consciousness, available for ordinary use.

The fourth and, for our purposes, the last fundamental fact is that each body is affected by the embodied consciousness and affects it long before it is sufficiently organized to convey to that consciousness definite information as to the world from which its materials were drawn. We may notice this to a very considerable extent if we watch the workings of the waking consciousness in a new infantile body. The consciousness answers to the discomfort of the body — from want of food, pain, etc. — before it is able to obtain through that body any definite idea as to its surroundings or any grasp of its own relations to them. And the astral and mental bodies answer to changes in consciousness by changed vibrations for ages before they hand on to the consciousness definite news of the events that are taking place around them in their respective worlds. Hence communications constantly take place between the worlds in which the man is normally living without the man knowing anything of their passage; he becomes conscious of a thought only when it affects his physical brain, and knows nothing of its origin or of the course it has followed ere its arrival in his physical body.

Let us begin our study of communications between different worlds with the every-day constantly arriving communications, and thus establish ourselves thoroughly on the normal before we enquire into the abnormal. Just as the, to us, inappreciable interval between the touching of a hot plate with the tip of a finger and the withdrawal of the finger is occupied with the passage of a wave in the sensory nerves from the periphery to the brain and the passage of a return wave from the brain through the motor nerves to the periphery, so is there the passage of a vibratory wave from the physical matter to the astral and from the astral to the mental, and a corresponding change in consciousness; it is the consciousness which feels the pain of the burning, and memorizes the fact for future guidance; the communication has run inwards from the physical body through the astral to the mental, a communication from world to world. Similarly is the change in consciousness, the will to move the finger from the hot substance, the cause of a vibration in the matter of the mental body, and this causes a vibration in the astral body, and this in turn in the physical brain — a communication from world to world. In all processes of thinking, there is a series of changes of consciousness in the mental world, these are answered by a corresponding series of vibrations in the mental body; these cause a series of corresponding vibratory changes in the astral body, strengthened by the consciousness — the same consciousness, remember, in all the bodies — and these set up similar vibratory changes in the etheric part of the physical; these etheric vibrations are largely electrical in character, and affect the cells of the dense physical brain, setting up vibratory changes therein; here you have the normal communication between the worlds, going on repeatedly, continually, varied by the reverse process, where the initiative is from outside; something occurs in the outer world which starts such a series of changes, one of the senses receives a stimulus and a nervous wave is set up; it passes from the dense to etheric matter, or begins in the etheric, is answered by a change of consciousness, runs up through astral to mental, intensifying the change, and the consciousness receives and registers the communication.

It is not waste of time to place clearly before our minds that communications are constantly running up and down the ladder of our bodies, each body a step in the ladder, and each step in a different world. The maintenance of our mental balance and of our powers of reasoning and of judgment in the face of the abnormal is rendered very much more easy when we understand that the abnormal is only an extension of the normal. If a person feels that he is facing something strange and unknown, something that he is inclined to regard as supernatural, he loses too often both judgment and reasoning faculty; but if he understands that the phenomenon before him is only a subtler repetition of a familiar happening, he is then able to observe accurately and to reason sensibly and acutely. As M. Jourdain was astonished to find that in his ordinary conversations he was talking prose, so may the student be astonished to find that he is continually communicating from world to world. Your consciousness may turn its attention outwards in any world in which it possesses a body to serve as window; you may look out through your physical, astral or mental window, but life is always the same you that looks out, that receives impressions.

Let us consider the next class of communications. A person becomes conscious of a thought, or rather an impression, arising in his waking consciousness, rather vaguely and somewhat indeterminate, which he cannot relate to anything in his physical surroundings, and which does not seem to be originated in his own consciousness. It seems to him to come from outside, but it lacks the sharpness of definition to which he is accustomed in the presence of real objects. Such impressions as premonitions, warnings of danger, apparently causeless depression or elation, feelings as to the mental, moral or physical condition of friends, as to illness, death, misfortune, good fortune, etc., intimations which do not come with the clearness of the spoken word or written message, but none the less cause a change in consciousness — what are these ? They are due to impacts made upon the astral body in the astral world, impacts which set up vibrations in its matter and thus give rise to changes of consciousness. The absence of precision of definition is due to the lack of organization of the astral body, and its consequent incapacity to receive clear impressions. The physical body has been in process of organization for millions of years, and can receive sharply defined series of vibrations, and the consciousness through this immense period of time has been learning to relate impacts to objects, to analyze and co-ordinate impressions made on its body, and thus to understand their meaning. Experience has evolved it into an admirable vehicle and instrument of consciousness. But the astral body is in very different case. In every fairly civilized and educated person it is partially organized, sufficiently organized to receive and reproduce sequences of vibrations thrown upon it from the astral plane, but its special sense-organs — the whirling wheels, or chakrams — are not as yet generally evolved in such persons, and hence sharply defined impressions cannot be received.

With closed eyes you can distinguish between the light and the dark; if when the sun was shining on your eyelids, a hand were interposed and threw a shade over them, you would be conscious of the difference, but you would not discern the hand; or if shadows were thrown on a sheet, your open eyes would see the shadow-dance, but it would only imperfectly convey a story which you could easily gather from a drama acted by persons visible to sight; so is it with the astral body of the average educated man. If at some distance from you an event takes place of great interest to yourself, bringing to you joy or grief, or if some persons think strongly of you, the vibrations thereby set up in astral matter will be propagated through space, like a Marconi message, and will impinge on your astral body, setting up similar vibrations therein. But unless the astral sense-organs are developed, a sharply defined picture cannot be produced, and hence only a vague impression will be made on the consciousness. The astral body and the astral sense-organs differ as do the physical body and the physical sense-organs, although much more substitution is possible in the one than in the other. The astral bodies of the educated are fairly well developed in form and general constitution, but are poorly organized as regards the sense-organs. There are, however, in the astral body very well developed centers connected with the physical organs of the senses — a center connected with the eye, one with the ear, and so on. These are sometimes stimulated into action by violent vibrations in the astral body, and then we have the phenomenon of second sight, the vision of phantoms, wraiths, phantasms of living or dead persons. It is also possible to stimulate the physical senses, but in a rather unhealthy way, by stimulating these centers through their appropriate physical organs, as by crystal-gazing, the use of magic mirrors, and other similar means. In this way an extension of sight on the physical plane may be gained, or even of vision in the lower regions of the astral world. But this is not a gaining of astral senses, but an unhealthy stimulation of physical senses, causing an abnormal increase of sensitiveness in the astral centers to which they are attached. It is the law of nature that development comes from above, and the forces of evolution work from above and organize that which is below. Life organizes matter, matter does not produce life. The consciousness working in the astral world organizes the physical sense-organs; the consciousness working in the mental world organizes the astral sense-organs, and so on. There is a continual working of consciousness for the improvement and the refining of its lower vehicles. As your evolution proceeds from the stage it has now reached with the most thoughtful and cultured persons, it is possible to quicken the unfolding of the astral senses by strenuous and clear thinking and by purity of desire and action; as these become active the communications received through the astral body will become clear and definite, like those received through the physical body. These are blurred now because the instrument is imperfect.

As the consciousness unfolds on plane after plane, in world after world, and organizes its vehicles in the world below that on which its own center is established, the lower bodies for all practical purposes unite into one body; if a person have the center of consciousness established on the mental plane, the astral and physical bodies function as a single body, and he lives consciously in two worlds. In the high consciousness of Those whom we call Masters all the worlds are to Them as one world in which Their waking consciousness is ever functioning, and They focus Their attention at any point without leaving the physical body. The worlds on which attention is not fixed are out of focus but are not invisible. When we are using physical sight only, things we are looking at are clear and distinct; the surrounding things are visible but not clearly defined. So if a man be living in two worlds, physical and astral things intermingle in his normal field of vision, but if he looks at the physical the astral is out of focus, if he looks at the astral the physical is out of focus. But a communication from any world can reach a Master, and by focusing his attention on it He sees the world from which it comes, and can, if He so will, answer it by sending the reply through the appropriate body. All His bodies function as one body for His consciousness, but each is there, a perfect instrument for action in any world. We, who have not reached that high perfection, may have to move from world to world, or leave one body to function in another; or, if we have passed that elementary stage of the higher evolution, we may have partly unified our lower bodies, and may be able to function on some planes as the Master does on all those which are manifested. Then, by paying attention to any message, we can know from what world it comes; it is all a question of the development of our bodies, the one consciousness receiving impressions from any world in which it is using a well-organized body. The whole question, therefore, is one of evolution — the unfolding of consciousness, the organization of bodies.

But there are many forms of communication that do not depend wholly on ourselves, forms used by other persons who desire to communicate with us, and which demand no growth on our own part, communications which present themselves to our normal consciousness in the physical body, and are surrounded with more or less of difficulty and danger because of the letting loose of forces, not usually employed on the physical plane, by the person making the communication. It is to these that we will next turn, remarking only that it is our own want of development that makes necessary the employment of these means, that forces more highly evolved Beings to come down to our level because we are not able to rise to Theirs.

It may be taken for granted as a general rule that no Being who is functioning on higher planes will go to a great expenditure of energy to manifest Himself physically at a point far removed from that at which His physical body is living, if He can do the work He needs to accomplish without such manifestation. He will always use the smallest amount of power necessary to achieve the aim He sets before Himself; He will take the easiest way, employ the easiest method; if the person with whom He wishes to communicate has so organized his higher bodies as to be able to receive communications on the subtler planes, then most certainly He will not go to the expenditure of energy necessary for appearance on the physical. Still it is sometimes necessary, and in olden times it was usual, for a Master to teach on the physical plane when His physical body was far away from the place at which the teaching was to be given. In such case the question arose, and arises: "What is the best method of communication?"

The Ancients answered this question in a simple and definite way. They said, and truly said, that the best method of communication was to use a pure, carefully trained and carefully guarded body, highly organized as to the nervous system, from which the legitimate owner could easily step out, or be sent out, leaving this body an empty tabernacle into which the Teacher - whose own physical body was far away — could step, and use it as His own. Such a body is like a well-made garment out of which the owner can slip, leaving it to be put on and worn by another. If a body is to be thus used, it is necessary that it should be guarded with scrupulous care; the surroundings should be beautiful and peaceful;

no rough or jarring vibrations should be allowed to ruffle the atmosphere; coarse and impure persons should not be allowed to approach it; its diet should be non-stimulating, nutritive and free from all products of ferment and decay; careful physical culture should preserve it in health. In the ancient Temples, ruled by those who were themselves Initiates of the lower or higher Mysteries, such bodies were to be found — those of the Vestal Virgins, or Sybils. These Virgins were originally young girls brought up with extreme care within the Temple precincts, and allowed to come into touch only with those who were pure and noble, and such a Virgin would be chosen as the means of communication. Seated on a stool or chair isolated from the earth's magnetism, the girl would leave her body — if trained to do so at will — or she would be thrown into a trance; then a Master, or a high Initiate, would take possession of the body, and through it teach the disciples gathered for instruction. That was the favourite way of teaching among the Ancients, and it was a good way, for it caused little disturbance of normal, physical forces; it merely afforded to a higher Being a vehicle which He could use, while the Vestal was no more disturbed than by an ordinary going to sleep. This was the way in which Pythagoras was wont to give instruction to His disciples in more lives than one.

In modern days such an organism is spoken of as that of a medium, and the lack of knowledge has brought about a degradation of the office; a person who is born a sensitive is taught to be passive, allows himself to be thrown into a trance and his body to be taken possession of, without knowledge of the entity who is going to use it, without discrimination or power of self-defense. Such persons usually pollute their bodies with flesh and alcohol, meet all people indiscriminately, allow anyone to sit with them, live amid sordid surroundings. The results are naturally trivial or repulsive. For this one cannot blame the mediums; it is ignorance which leads to such conditions. If Mr. Stead be able to carry out the plan that he and his astral-world friend Miss Ames — Julia — have formed, he will raise the medium to a far higher position, will guard sensitives from evil surroundings, and will fence his séance-room against undesirable intruders belonging both to the physical and astral worlds. Julia's Bureau is the first attempt in modern days to open systematic and carefully guarded channels of communication between the living and super-living along this particular line; nor are the absent living excluded from using it, if they are able to go thither in their astral bodies.

In our own days, H. P. Blavatsky was largely used by her Master and other Teachers as such a means of communication. She was a most extraordinary and rare compound. Her body and nervous system were of the most sensitive type; she was born a medium, and was surrounded during her childhood and youth by a wealth of mediumistic phenomena. But she had also an intelligence of extraordinary vividness and a will of steel. Rarely indeed is such a combination found, but it was ideal for an occultist; in fact, a Master said that no such body had been available for two hundred years. Her character was positive and imperious, and her occult training made even stronger her already strong will. Throughout her life as one of the Founders of the Theosophical Society, she was constantly stepping out of the physical body, in order to place it at the service of her own Master or at that of one of the Teachers, the face and voice sometimes so much changing as to bewilder unaccustomed spectators. Colonel Olcott has told us in his Old Diary Leaves that most of his own occult instruction reached him in this ancient way; she would step out of her body, a Master would step in, and through her lips would teach the eager, devoted disciple. Of all ways of communicating, as I said above, this is the best, because it causes least disturbance; but there are few people who are fit to serve as such a channel. Not understanding the conditions necessary to make the body fit for the use of a Being on the level of a Master, people do not train and keep their bodies sufficiently well to be used in this way, and for the most part what is done now-a-days along these lines is not of the nature of possession but rather of inspiration, when the mind is raised above its normal level by contact with the mind of the Master, and some of His thought flows through it.

The very opposite of this means of communication, as dangerous as the other is safe, is where a materialization of a physical body is brought about. Our Masters have used also this method, and in the early days of the Theosophical Society it was not infrequently employed. The Master comes in His mãyãvî rûpã — phantasmal body — and densifies it on the spot where He chooses to appear by drawing out of the atmosphere, or out of the body of some one present, the particles which, built into the subtle body, make it visible and sometimes tangible. Colonel Olcott saw his Master first in this way in New York; so also I saw Him for the first time in Fontainebleau in 1889. In this way several of the Masters and of Their initiated disciples have appeared to members of the Theosophical Society. Mr. Leadbeater, Damodar, Pandit Bhavani Shankar, Mr. Subbiah Chetty, are some of the various witnesses of such appearances at Adyar and elsewhere.

The question will naturally be asked: Why should so impressive and satisfactory a means of communication be dangerous ? Because of the universality of the well-known law that "action and re-action are equal and opposite." Whenever the forces of the higher planes are caused to affect the lower directly, there is a re-action equal to the action caused, and the direct action down here of a Brother of the White Lodge is followed by a similar direct action here of a Brother of the Dark Lodge. One of the Masters in an early letter explained this dangerous re-action from the phenomena worked by H. P. Blavatsky, and the destructive results on those around her, and many of us have seen plenty of confirmation of the law. Wherever these manifestations of force occur there is storm and trouble, and those who seem, at the moment, to be most highly favoured are those on whom falls the weight of the inevitable recoil. They suffer physically or mentally, there is loss of equilibrium or nervous disturbance. The nervous strain to which H. P. Blavatsky was subjected by the wealth of phenomena produced by her broke down her physical health and aged her before her time. And it is noteworthy that because of the strain involved by this play of forces in the life of discipleship, physical health has ever been in the East a condition of discipleship.

Biographies of seers, of saints, are full of evidence of the working of this law, and without definite training no physical body can stand the strain of psychic experiences. So constantly have hysteria and seership been found together that some regard all exhibitions of seership as resulting from disturbance of mental equilibrium, and it is true in very many cases that psychic sensitiveness and overstrained nerves go together. Magnetic, electrical and other forms of etheric vibrations are set up on the physical plane with the exhibition of the subtler forces, and unless people within their reach know how to protect themselves they pay for their presence in disordered nerves and strained brains.

Another means of communication is the sending of a message by the Master through a disciple. Such a message would often be given by the disciple in his Master's form. For astral and mental bodies follow the thought of their wearers, and if the disciple bearing the message is thinking intently on his Master, his body might assume His appearance and the sender of the message would appear as its deliverer. The mental or astral body assuming that form, the denser material built into it would also follow it, and thus an appearance of the Master might take place although He Himself was not present.

Similarly, again, a thought-form of the Master might bring the communication, and that happens more frequently than the actual coming of the Master to any particular place. It has been observed, quite apart from any question of a Master, that one person will see the form of another where only a thought-form had been sent, and no visit had been paid in the astral body. A person whose mind has been fairly well-trained may send such a thought-form, and it will assume the form of the sender. I have myself very often been told that I had appeared in particular places and had done certain actions, and those who had seen the phantasm were not easily to be convinced that I had not paid them any visit but had only thought of them. If the percipient had been trained to close observation, he would have been able to distinguish between a thought-form and a person, but in the absence of such training a person may say quite honestly: I saw my friend, when he had only seen his friend's thought-form.

Moreover, it is possible for a person to project a thought-form and then to perceive it as an external object. A Master might send a thought to a student, and thus bring about a change of consciousness in that student on the higher levels of the mental plane. That change of consciousness caused by the Master will bring about corresponding vibrations in the student's causal body, and these will be reproduced in the normal way in the mental and astral bodies and thus carried to the etheric; a person most readily affected through the auditory nerves might under such circumstances hear the Master's voice, and hear it either inside or outside his brain; one most readily affected through the optic nerves might equally see the Master's form; each might believe that he had heard or seen the Master Himself, when he had unconsciously manufactured in his etheric brain the voice or the form. In such cases the communication would be a real one, but the shape it would take on the physical plane would be illusory.

It is stated in the Acts of the Apostles that when the Holy Spirit came down upon the twelve, every one in the assembled crowd heard them speak in his own tongue. To the person who does not understand matters such as those with which this article deals, the story seems incredible. Yet it is not so. For the thought of the Apostles caused in each hearer a mental change, reproducing itself in the mind of each; that change became each man's thought, and reached each man's brain in the ordinary way; there it clothed itself in words, the words into which each man was accustomed daily unconsciously to translate his own thoughts. The man thought that he heard the Apostles speaking words in his own language, whereas they spoke in thoughts and he translated them into his own tongue. Similarly, if a worker on the astral plane finds that he cannot communicate with some one whom he desires to help through the medium of a common language, he will — if he have learned to use his mental body — transmit the thought to the mind of his companion, leaving him to translate the mental image into his own language. He does the translation, but he will consider that his friend has spoken to him, whereas he has only received from him a mental impression which he has himself translated after his accustomed fashion. That wonted interaction of mind and brain, the normal translation of mental image into words, is used by those working on higher planes as offering a convenient means of communication, with those on lower planes, who use a language unknown to themselves. Thus an eastern Master, not knowing English, will " speak in English " to a western pupil. He may even write it by taking from the pupil's brain the words He needs.

There is one other possibility that should not be omitted: the personification of a Brother of the Light by a Brother of the Shadow or of a disciple of the one by a disciple of the other. It may happen that for the deceiving of a person possessing wide influence, and the consequent harm that may be wrought by such a one when deceived, a Brother of the Shadow may personate a White Brother, and give a mischievous order or direction. In such a case everything depends at first on the intuition of the one whom it is sought to mislead, and then the matter passes on to the intuition and judgment of others. Should such a possibility be before the Society, each member must form his own opinion on the veracity and reliability of the communication, after considering all the circumstances of the case, the knowledge and the character of the supposed victim, the bearing of the communication on the welfare of the Society, and all collateral happenings. Sometimes the question can be finally decided only after the expiry of a considerable period of time; thus in the case of the Judge secession, time has spoken by the continuance and growth of the original Society, its output of literature, its increasing vitality and power, compared with the breaking up of the secession into various smaller bodies, the decrease in adherents, the paucity of literature, the small influence on the public. Time proves all things, and its verdict is without appeal. So will it be with the controversy aroused by the Adyar manifestations. In patience possess ye your souls, and after using your best judgment await that verdict. The fire of time proves all things; it burns up dross and leaves the gold purified and resplendent. The Lord of the Burning-Ground throws all things earthly into His fires; let us await the results without fear, willing that our dross shall be consumed and hoping that some pure gold may, in the end, remain.

It will be evident to those who consider these various means of communication that it is well-nigh impossible for persons at a distance from the place where a communication had been made to decide on the form it may have taken, unless they have at their command occult methods of investigation. The nature of the manifestations which took place at Adyar in the winter of 1906-1907 could not be decided by the ordinary member of the Society, unversed in occult phenomena. He was forced either to rely on the good faith and accuracy of those present during their occurrence or able to study them occultly, or to suspend his judgment. The data were insufficient for an independent decision in the matter. And such is the case with regard to most of the phenomena which have occurred in the history of the Society. Unless we can accept the good faith and the competence of the witnesses, or have the power to investigate the past for ourselves, we must perforce suspend our judgment. Irrational credulity and irrational incredulity are both signs of an unbalanced mind, and, where evidence sufficient to satisfy us is lacking, our right course is to abstain alike from affirmation and denial. It is clear that in such matters each must decide for himself, and that none has the right to dictate how any other member shall think. A person who has definite knowledge may affirm that such and such a thing happened, but he cannot claim authority to impose his knowledge on others as sufficient proof of the happening, nor should he blame them if they deny his competence as a witness. The entire freedom of each member to exercise his own reason on these matters is necessary to the security and progress of the Society.

The paucity of communications permitted to be made public during many years was a proof of the want of balance, judgment, common-sense and calmness in the general Society. People had come to regard communications from the Masters with doubt, suspicion and fear, and consequently, as they caused much turmoil, they were withheld, save when absolutely necessary. In the earlier days they were common because the fact of the open door was very generally recognized. Now they are rare, because of the turmoil they cause. But if we believed what theoretically most of us accept, that we are living in three worlds all the time and are related to those worlds by the inclusion of their matter in our body, we should regard it as natural, not unnatural, that we should receive by way of our appropriated matter impacts from each of the three worlds. On our receptiveness, not on these outer worlds, depends our knowledge of them and our communication with them.

It is all-important for the progress of the Society that, however true the fact of communication between these worlds, neither the fact itself, nor any particular instance of it, should be imposed upon the members of the Society by authority, either open or tacit. Each member must be left free to accept or reject on his own responsibility that which is affirmed by any other. If, in the exercise of this discretion, a member rejects what is true, that is his own loss, and it is far better that he should lose than that the Society should be deprived of the liberty which keeps open the path of progress. If a majority of the Society rejected a true and important communication, a communication from a Master, then the Society would perish as an organization, and the minority would be left to carry on the work. That was the peril in which the Theosophical Society stood after the manifestations at Adyar, and the expression to Colonel Olcott of the Master's wish as to the nomination of his successor. But the great majority of the Society obeyed the Master's wish, and the danger was averted.

Such a peril might again confront us, but we must not buy security from it by restricting the freedom of members to think for themselves. Every member must be left free to believe or not to believe. None has the right to say: "I believe it, therefore you must accept it". None has the right to say: "I do not believe it, therefore you must reject it". There is no coercion in saying: "I know this to be true" any more than there is coercion in saying: " I know that putting those substances together will form an explosive compound"; if anyone chooses to put them together then he will find out by his own experience that such a compound is formed. As a Master once said when He was accused of uttering a threat because He stated what would follow a certain line of action: " A warning is not a threat." Elder students may see a danger that younger students do not see, and they are sometimes bound to put their knowledge at the service of the younger; but the younger must be left free to accept or to reject the warning, and in the latter case to buy their own experience at the cost of suffering that would have been avoided by utilizing the experience of their elders. Progress is made along both lines and is, for the most part, gained by a blending of the two methods. The laws of nature do not change because we are ignorant of them, and if we make a mistake, however conscientiously, we shall suffer as we strike against the law. The conscientious decision will improve our character, and our knowledge will be increased by our experience. Those who have already gained that knowledge may rightly offer it to their fellows though they may not impose it on them, otherwise would they lay themselves open to the reproach: " You knew we were ignorantly running into danger; why did you not warn us ? "

`The Theosophical Society, as the nucleus of the Coming Race, must encourage variety of opinion within its borders, in order that it may gather up within itself all seeds of truth, even though they be enclosed within husks of error. The husk will drop away and the seed will remain and grow. The Society will never be destroyed by varieties of thought, if only we practice perfect tolerance, and put no barrier in the way of freedom of expression. But do not let us encourage negations while discouraging affirmations, lest we should grow towards the darkness rather than towards the light.

`While we guard liberty of thought and expression and encourage the fullest discussion of differences, let us not forget courtesy and gentleness, lest difference of thought should glide into vituperation of those who think differently from ourselves. Personal attack and imputation of evil motives are the weapons of attack used by the uncultured and the vulgar, and should find no place in Theosophical discussion. Love is as vital as knowledge for the growth of the future, and the knowledge which is without love is useless to the Master-Builders of the Coming Race.

THE REALITY OF THE INVISIBLE AND THE ACTUALITY OF THE UNSEEN WORLDS

by Annie Besant

THE majority of civilized people today, in every country, profess a belief in the existence of worlds other than the physical globes scattered through space, the suns and planets of our own and other systems. However vague may be their ideas of the nature of such worlds, invisible, superphysical, super-sensuous; however much the ideas vary, according to the religion professed by the believer; they yet cling to a belief that not all of me shall die, that death does not put an end to individual existence, that there is something beyond the tomb. But if we estimate the value of the belief by the criterion suggested by Professor Bain, that the strength of a belief may be tested by the influence it exerts over conduct, then we find that, despite the nominal profession, the belief itself is of the flimsiest character. The conduct of people is ruled by their belief in the visible world rather than in those invisible; their thoughts, interests, affections, all center here; and so markedly is this the case that the behavior of anyone who is really influenced by the thought of the superphysical worlds is deemed eccentric and morbid. A patient's body may be worn out by extreme old age, or tortured by a disease that must shortly end in death; doctors, nurses, relatives, will strain every nerve to scourge the will to hold on to the useless body, will pour into it drugs and stimulants to put off for a few days or weeks its dissolution, as though the life beyond this world were a mirage, or a thing to be avoided as long as possible by every means. This lack of the sense of the actuality of the superphysical worlds is more common in modern than in ancient times, in the West than in the East. Its wide prevalence is due to the conception of man as a being who possesses no present relation with those worlds, and no powers which would enable him to cognize them. Man is regarded as living in one world, the world of waking consciousness, the world of the triumphs of the senses and the intellect, instead of in several worlds, in all of which his consciousness is functioning, more or less definitely; he is no longer supposed to possess the powers which all religions have ascribed to him, powers which transcend the limitations of the body; and the active Agnosticism of the scientist, of the leaders of thought, is reflected in the passive Agnosticism of the intellectual masses, whose lip-belief in the superphysical is mocked by the conduct-belief of ordinary life.

It is not enough that we should think of the super-physical worlds as worlds that we may, or even shall, pass into after death; the realization of these worlds, if they are to influence conduct, must be a constant fact in consciousness, and man must live consciously in the three worlds, the physical, the astral, the heavenly. For that only is actual to man to which his consciousness responds; if his consciousness does not answer to a thing, for him that thing has no existence; the boundary of his power to respond is the boundary of his recognition of the existent. A man might be surrounded by the play of colors, but were it not for the eye, they would not, for him, exist; waves of melody might sweep around him, but without the ear, there would, for him, be silence. And so the worlds invisible may play on a man, but while he is unconscious of their presence, for him they do not exist. So long as that irresponsiveness continues, no amount of description can make them living, actual; to him they must remain as the dream of the poet, the vision of the painter, the hope of the optimist, beautiful exceedingly, perchance, but without proof, without substance, without reality. But can the invisible worlds be made present in consciousness, can we respond to them, and share their life ? Are there in man powers not yet unfolded, but to be unfolded in evolution, so that he may be likened to a flower not yet opened, powers that lie hidden like the stamens, the petals, in the bud ? Are the Prophets, the Saints, the Mystics, the Seers, the men in whom these possibilities have flowered, and are their methods of prayer or of meditation the scientific means of culture which hasten the unfolding of the bud ?

In seeking to answer this question we may look back into the past or analyze the present, we may study the religions of ancient times, or we may scrutinize our own constitution and seek to understand its constituents and the relations of these to our environment. Along these lines, it may be, some results may be obtained.

Looking back over the religions of the past we find one idea dominating them all — that the visible universe is the reflection of the invisible. Egypt sees the world of phenomena as the image of the real world. To India the universe is but the passing expression of a divine Idea; there is but one Reality, and the universe is its shadow. The Hebrews in their philosophic books assert that God made the universe of Ideas before the universe of forms; the celestial man, Adam Kadmon, is the original, whereof the terrestrial man is the copy, and Philo says that God, intending to make the visible universe, first created the invisible; in the Talmud it is regarded as axiomatic that if a man would know the invisible he should study the visible, and the Hebrew Paul declares that the invisible things are plainly seen by those that are made. Pythagoras tells of the world of Ideas, and has real forms existing in the intelligible world, the world of Ideas in the Universal Mind, ere the Ideas were manifested as the physical universe. So again Plato and his followers. Everywhere is this dominating thought, that there is an invisible which is real, and a visible which is unreal, a copy, a reflection. Only the Real is eternal, and only the eternal can satisfy, since Thou art That . The Real manifests as the unreal, the Eternal masks itself as the transitory; how strange the paradox, how complete the subversion, when the unreal is considered to be the only reality, and the transitory the only existence.

During the immense period of time covered by these and by other religions, man was regarded as an immortal consciousness veiled in matter, the consciousness becoming more and more limited as the veils of matter grew thicker and thicker; his deepest relations were with the world of Ideas, and each world grew more unreal, more illusory, as the matter which composed it grew more and more dense and gross. The phenomenal worlds were, as their name denotes, worlds of appearances, not of realities, and man must pierce through these appearances to reach the core of Reality. This Spirit endued the garment of mind, and over the mind the garb of the senses, in order to come into relation with the intellectual and sensuous worlds, and man, the resulting composite, must rise above the senses, must transcend the mind, in order to be self-consciously Spirit. As in himself as Spirit he knows the spiritual, so in his mind-garment he knows the intellectual, in his sense-garment the sensuous.

The sense-garment is threefold, and each layer relates him to a material world — the heavenly, the astral, the physical. All these are truly visible, each cognizable through sense-organs composed of its own state of matter, but only the grossest is visible to the normal man, because in him only the grossest layer of the sense-garment is in thorough working order. As the finer layers of the sense-garment are gradually evolved into similar working order, the finer phenomenal worlds will become sensuous to him, tangible to his senses. Thus was it taught in elder days; thus is it now taught in

Theosophy. The pseudo-invisible — that which is capable of being seen although invisible to the eyes of the flesh — will become visible as evolution proceeds, bringing into functioning activity the finer layers of our sense-garment, and then the three worlds will become the visible universe. Such functioning activity may even be brought about, at the present stage of evolution, by special methods, and man may live consciously in the three worlds at once. For such men the actuality of the lower invisible worlds is established on that so-called indubitable evidence, the evidence of the senses, and it is of this sensuous evolution that many, perhaps most, people think when they speak of obtaining proof of the persistence of individual consciousness on the other side of death. Such evidence, however, must remain for a considerable time to come out of the reach of the majority of people, although the minority able to obtain it is ever-increasing and is certain to increase more rapidly in the coming years. The available evidence for the existence of the finer layers of the sense-garment, and for man's relations through it with superphysical worlds, is abundant and is continuously receiving additions. Clairvoyance, clairaudience, premonitions, warning and prophetic dreams, apparition of doubles, thought-forms and astral bodies, etc., etc., are beginning to play a part in ordinary life and to find unjeering reportal in the daily press. Signs of evolving sense-organs are thus around us, and the unimportance of death will be more and more recognized as these multiply. It is no longer possible for a person, instructed in the well-ascertained facts of mesmeric and hypnotic trances, to regard mental faculties as the products of nervous cells. It is known that the working of those cells may be paralyzed while perception, memory, reason, imagination, manifest themselves more potently, with wider range and fuller powers. Those who have patiently and steadily observed the phenomena occurring at spiritualistic séances know that when every doubtful happening is thrown aside, there remains a residuum of undoubted facts which prove the presence of forces unknown to science, and of intelligence that is not from the sitters or the medium. Automatic writing has been carried to a point where the agent concerned cannot be the brain-consciousness of the writer. Thought-transference — telepathy — has passed beyond the range of controversy and has established itself as a fact by reiterated and exact proofs. The worlds unseen are becoming the seen, and their forces are asserting themselves in the physical world by the production of effects not generated by physical causes. The boundaries of the known are being pushed back until they begin to overlap those of the astral world. The evidence increases so rapidly that the materialist of forty years ago threatens to become as extinct as the dodo, and the whole attitude of the intellectual classes to life is changing. And yet, amidst all this, it may be well for us to realize that these extensions of knowledge, valuable as they are, can only, at the best, give us proofs of a prolongation of life, not of our immortality, for the three worlds are all phenomenal, all changing, and therefore all transitory. They add to our physical life, an astral life and a heavenly life; they give us three visible worlds instead of one; they enlarge our horizons, and add to our material inheritance; they do not, and they cannot, give us the certitude of immortality.

To say this is not to undervalue the further improvement of our sense-garment, but to put the senses in their right place as regards our knowledge of the superphysical worlds, even as we have learned to put them in their right place in our knowledge of the physical. If we analyse carefully the knowledge which we gain through observation every day and at once utilise for our conduct, we find that very little of it is directly obtained through the senses; at our present stage of physical evolution the experiment to prove this is not quite easy, but it is not impossible. If we would make the experiment we must proceed as follows; we shut out all that the mind has deduced from previous observations, and narrow ourselves down to pure sensuous perception of an object, such as a face, a landscape; we mark only what the eye reports, and as far as possible add nothing to that sensation from the mind that has perceived, noted, registered, compared, so many previous similar sensations; we see, as an infant sees, outline and colour, with no distance, no depth, no relations between adjoining parts, no meaning. When we now look over a landscape, we see into it countless observations, movements and experiences made from our babyhood upwards; the infant's eye is as perfect as our own, but does not measure the near and the far, the relation of parts that makes a whole. When the eye sees under quite new conditions it is easy to deceive it; the senses are continually corrected and supplemented by the mind. Now when first the finer sense-organs of our sense-garment begin to work, they are as the eyes of the infant on the physical plane, but behind them is an actively functioning mature mind, full of ideas built up out of physical-plane sensations; this content it throws into the outline supplied by the astral sense-organ, and the man "sees" an astral object; as on the physical plane, by far the greater part of the perception is mind-supplied, but while the mind on the physical plane supplies details collected by countless physical-plane observations of similar objects, and thus adds to the sense-report its own store of congruous memories, the mind on the astral plane projects into the sense-perception the same store of memories, now incongruous, for it lacks the astral observations which should form its contribution to the total perception. There is a fertile source of error, continually overlooked, and hence early observations are most misleading, and the observations of the untrained continue to be earth-filled.

In order that we may be sure of our immortality, something quite other than this refining of the sense-garment is necessary, something that is related to life and not to life-vehicles. We may climb rung after rung of the world's ladder, and yet remain unsatisfied; for infinities stretch ever above us as below us infinities stretch, and stunned, dwarfed by the immensities above and below, it seems to matter little whether we occupy one rung or another of the ladder. This is ever going outwards, adding one mass of phenomena to another mass, a true weaving of endless ropes out of illimitable sand. And if the Word of the Mystics be true we must turn inwards, not outwards, when we would seek wisdom instead of learning. It is indeed obvious that no extension, no refinement of the senses can introduce us into worlds really invisible, into that which is not phenomenal, into the world of thought, not the world of thought-forms. For this the consciousness must unfold the powers ever within it, and make manifest the divinity which is its hidden nature. Consciousness is the Real, conditioned by matter, and we must plunge into the depths of our own being if we would find the certitude of immortality in conscious union with the One. All other proofs are supplementary; this is primary and final, the Alpha and Omega of life. Consciousness is the Ever-Invisible: "Not in the sight abides his form; none may by the eye behold him"; yet herein resides the full certainty of the Reality of the Ever-Invisible, of that which escapes alike the senses and the mind. As the eye responds to light, the ear to sound, the material to the material, so must consciousness learn to respond to consciousness, the spiritual to the spiritual. When this is learned, the question of death can never more distress us, nor doubt of the necessary existence of worlds for the continued life of the imperfect discarnate assail us; for when consciousness realises its own inherent immortality, it knows itself essentially independent of the three worlds, a spiritual entity belonging to a spiritual world.

The answer to the question: "Can we know this, not only hope it ?" comes alike from religion and from philosophy. The greatest of our humanity declare that this knowledge is within the reach of man; it is the Brahmavidyã, the Gnosis, Theosophy. And the ancient narrow path along which men have trodden from times immemorial, along which have gone the teachers of every religion and the disciples that have followed in their footsteps, that ancient narrow path is as open for the treading of men today as it was open to the men of the past. The human Self is as divine in the twentieth century as in the first, or as in thousands of years before; the life of God is as near to the human Spirit. For the Spirit is the offspring, the emanation of Deity, and it can know because it is like its Parent. It is said in an ancient writing that the proof of God is the conviction in the human Self; that is the one priceless evidence, that testimony to the divine Reality which comes from the Real in us. Hence man may know the Reality of the Ever-Invisible, as well as the Actuality of the, at present, invisible worlds.

In search of this testimony Religion bids the believer tread the road of Prayer. By intense concentrated prayer, when the life is pure, a man may so rend the sense-garment that Spirit may commingle with Spirit, the human with the divine. The rapt ecstasy of prayer may lift the devotee to the Object of devotion, and he may feel the bliss of union, the ineffable joy of the Lord. Never again may he doubt the reality of that high communion. And, far short of this, the man of prayer may have experience of the inner worlds, may feel their peace, their joy, may bask in their light. These experiences are facts in consciousness, and lift the man beyond all possibility of doubt as to the Reality of the Invisible. To call them subjective, to talk of the reflex action of prayer, does not explain nor destroy their value. That the consciousness may be widened, uplifted, illuminated, is the all-important fact; the man feels himself in touch with a fuller consciousness, an up-welling life; his hunger is appeased, and the food reaches him from realms that are not physical. Along this road of prayer he may reach sureness of the existence of the invisible. For the simple, the devotional, this path is the easier to tread.

There is another road to which Philosophy points, in which man turns inwards, not outwards, and finds certitude of Reality within himself. The one certainty for each of us, needing no proof, beyond all argument, incapable of being strengthened by any act of the reason, is the sure truth: I am. This is the ultimate fact of consciousness, the foundation on which everything else is built. All save that is inference. We argue the existence of matter from changes produced in our consciousness by other than ourselves; we argue the existence of people around us from the sensations we receive from them. All is inference save the one central fact of consciousness; all else changes, but that never. In that stability, that changelessness, is the mark of the Real; the Real is the changeless, the eternal, and this one changeless thing is the Real ingarbed in form.

If, studying man in his present stage of evolution, we seek to know the seat of this Self-consciousness, we find that in most of us its throne is the lower mind. In truth, the place in evolution of each conscious being may be judged by the recognition of the seat of consciousness. If that seat be in the physical body, we find consciousness, but not Self-consciousness; there is not there the power of distinguishing the " I " from the impact of impressions causing sensations. Higher in the ladder of being, consciousness is seated in the second layer of the sense-garment, and this is the case with animals and with large classes of men. The life with which these identify themselves is the life of sensations, and of the thoughts which serve sensations; from this they gradually rise to a consciousness which identifies itself with the mind, which has risen from the life of sensations to the life of thought. From this life of the lower mind, in which sensations still play so large a part, man rises to the life of the intellect, and the lower mind becomes his instrument, ceasing to be himself. From the life of the intellect he must rise to the life of the Spirit, and know himself as the One. The seat of Self-consciousness is moved from the lower mind to the higher by strenuous thinking, by the intellectual travail of the student, the philosopher, the man of science — if the latter turn his thoughts from objects to principles, from phenomena to laws. And as strenuous thinking can alone lift the seat of Self-consciousness from the mind to the intellect, so can deep concentration and meditation alone raise that seat from the intellect to the Spirit.

The man who would deliberately quicken his own evolution must, having transcended the life of the senses, strive to make his life the life of the intelligence, rather than the life of mere outer activity. As he succeeds, he will become more, not less, effective in the outer world, for he will fulfil all his duties there with less of effort, with less dispersal of energy; a strength, a calmness, a serenity, a power of endurance, will be marked in him which will make him a more effective helper of others, and a more efficient worker in his daily tasks. While he discharges these faithfully, his true life will be within, and he will practise daily the higher powers of the intellect as they unfold; as these become familiar, he will gaze into the darkness beyond the intellect, seeking by concentrated meditation to find the light that is beyond the darkness, the light of the Real, of the Self. In that silence will arise within him the spiritual consciousness, responding to subtle thrillings from an unknown world. First feebly, and then more strongly, with a courage ever-increasing, that loftier consciousness answers to the without and realizes the within; he knows himself as Spirit; he knows himself divine.

To such a one all worlds are open; nature has no veil in all her kingdoms. The heavens spread around him, and living Selves, discarnate and incarnate, people the various worlds. He knows that death is nothing, that life is ever-evolving, not because he has seen with the finer organs of the sense-garment the astral and mental bodies which clothe the departed, and can thus view the unbroken continuity of life here and there, but because he knows consciousness as eternal, not subject to death. To him, the universe is rooted in life, and the changing forms are unimportant, since the Real is, however forms may change. This sure conviction needs no phenomenal proofs to make it more sure; it is based on the nature of things. The actuality of the unseen worlds is, indeed, known to him, but his rock is the Reality of the Ever-Invisible; all worlds are actual, because they are the masks of the Reality, but they might all fade away as shadows, and yet would the Real remain.

www.ingramcontent.com/pod-product-compliance
Lightning Source LLC
LaVergne TN
LVHW050947080826
845145LV00004B/1447

* 9 7 8 1 6 3 1 1 8 5 6 9 4 *